A 21-Day Journey to Freedom

FREE
YO
MIND

BREAKING THE CYCLES AND PATTERNS
OF LIMITED THINKING

JACQUE JAYE

Contents

Introduction v

Before You Start ix

Day 1	What Are Limits? 1
Day 2	What Are YOUR Limits? 5
Day 3	You Can Only See So Far 9
Day 4	Seeing Through God's Eyes 13
Day 5	Who Are You Surrounded By? 17
Day 6	The Failure To Communicate 21
Day 7	You Cannot Rescue You 25
Day 8	God Will Remember His Promises/Plans Concerning You 29
Day 9	God Will Come *See* About You 33
Day 10	God Can... God Will Rescue You 37
Day 11	You Must Come Out 41
Day 12	You Must Be Decided 45
Day 13	The Journey To Healing Begins 49
Day 14	What Is Faith? 53
Day 15	What Is Walking By Faith 57
Day 16	Prayer Time - Building Relationship With The LORD ... 61
Day 17	Your Mind Must Be Renewed 65
Day 18	Building Up Your Faith 69
Day 19	Stay Focus - Keep Your Eyes On The LORD 73
Day 20	You Are Not Alone 77
Day 21	Divine Connections 81

Closing Thoughts 85

About the Author 87

Introduction

First, I want to THANK YOU for purchasing this book!

What you hold in your hand is the outline of the *Journey to Freedom* Holy Spirit took me on. After almost nineteen years of marriage, I found myself starting life over. Then, I was hurt, angry and disappointed in myself regarding how I got to *that* place. I was hurt, angry and disappointed at God for not fixing *it*. And I was hurt, angry and disappointed at my ex-husband for failing me and our children. Not until I yielded completely to the Holy Spirit did these emotions begin to heal.

As I walked this path, I had to face myself. The broken me tucked behind different masks and the wall I erected to protect myself from further hurt, pain, and disappointment. On this path I had to answer some tough questions. I had to dig deep to answer the question most on my mind - how did I get *here*? As I walked with the Holy Spirit, I discovered so much about Him, myself, and our relationship. I also learned how my upbringing played a much greater part in my decision making than I realize. The journey was not easy, but it was well worth it.

This journal is designed to assist you in starting your *Journey to Freedom* in the LORD. Allow the Holy Spirit to lead you through this journal. Be patient with His way. The Holy Spirit only reveals an area that requires dealing once He knows you can handle the process of breaking and renewing in it. On this journey you will learn to trust Him like you never had before. Your eyes will begin to open, seeing life from a different perspective - the perspective of the Kingdom of God.

As you go through this book, always remember, your journey is **your** journey. It is designed specifically for you. Do not compare your process or progress to anyone else's, this will leave you confused, insecure and doubting the work of Holy Spirit in you. Keep your eyes on the LORD and eventually life as you know it will begin to reflect the change taking place inside of you.

Know this, the process is not a one-time thing, Holy Spirit has much work to do in all of us. Do not allow this to deter or discourage you. It is all a part of the process of becoming like Christ (2 Corinthians 3:18).

Before I close, may I suggest seeking counsel from your pastor, a licensed counselor and/or a trusted advisor if certain areas are too much for you to handle through prayer alone. Remember, you are human and as a human sometimes we need contact with other humans to help us navigate through life. Jesus is all; however, He provided these people to help us along our earthly journey.

Lastly, it is my prayer for you to stay the course. I pray that you embrace the complete work of Holy Spirit in your life. I pray that you too come to know the joy of living life free.

Your Friend In Christ,

Jacque Jaye

I give all praise to my LORD and Savior, Jesus
Christ, for the book you hold in your hand!

Not only did He never give up on me. He led me on my
Journey to Freedom. He also walked me through writing this
book. I love You more than I could ever express in words.

I prayerfully submit this work back to You ~ let
Your will be done on earth as it is in heaven.

Before You Start

Many desire freedom from the life of limits [bondage] they are living in, but do not know where or how to start. The book in your hand is your personal journal to help jumpstart this process. The *Journey to Freedom* is not always easy, however the liberation you will experience will be well worth it.

The journey to freedom requires three things from you:

1. Commitment
    a. You must decide to go all the way through the 21 days and beyond - no matter what.
2. Honesty
    a. You must be honest with yourself - God cannot deal with nor heal the areas of your life you are unwilling to confess and/or yield to Him.
3. Willingness
    a. You must be willing to do the work.

I strongly recommend you complete one lesson a day in chronological order as each day builds on the last. Take your time on this journey, it may take 21 days for one person and 63 for the next. It cannot be stressed enough, this is **your** *Journey to Freedom*, allow Holy Spirit to minister to you as needed.

You can use this book for personal study, or you can partner with others who have the same desire to *Journey to Freedom*. My hope is that you will read each Scripture and carefully consider each question and/or thought presented. To get the most from this journey, I strongly suggest

you be honest with yourself. Do not answer the questions with 'safe' answers, take the mask off and prayerfully answer the questions after a true assessment of yourself – how you really think and feel. Remember, God cannot deal with nor heal the areas of your life you are unwilling to confess and/or yield to Him.

Be sure to have a bible on hand to read the scriptures provided to further enhance each days thought points. I suggest using various translation of the bible to gain greater understanding of the verse.

May I pray for you…

Father God, in the name of Jesus, I pray for the person holding this book. As they prepare to start this journey, I ask You to provide them with strength to endure the process. I pray they stay on the course until it is completed. Even now, I come against the planned attacks of Satan and his army to cast doubt, discouragement, and fear. I pray they utilize their helmet of salvation. That it will be intact to block the thoughts coming against their minds that do not align with Your work in this hour. Father, may they have their shield of faith readily available as needed to thwart the fiery darts of the enemy in attempt to stop them on their path. I pray Father, they begin to find joy in You and in Your Kingdom as their minds are being renewed. Father, let Your will be done, in Jesus mighty name. Amen.

Let the
Journey Begin!

What Are Limits?

Limits ~ something that bounds, restrains or confines.
Limited ~ confined within limits.

Limits Hinder The Work of God

Read: Genesis 2:9; Deuteronomy 30:1; Joshua 24:15
Think About It: How has your power to choose hindered you?

_____

_____

_____

_____

_____

We Serve A Limitless God

Read: Genesis 1:1; John 1:3
Think About It: Do you believe God's resources
are limitless? Why or why not?

_____

_____

_____

_____

_____

Further Thought: Limits tell us, "You can only go so far."
Think About It: How has this belief affected your life?

_____

_____

_____

_____

_____

Tying It All Together:

For so long we have been living within limits. The safe and comfortable place we built to protect ourselves from hurt, disappointment and betrayal. This not the life God designed for us. He wants us to live a life of love, joy, and freedom. He has so much planned for us beyond the limits we have caged ourselves in.

NOTES

What Are YOUR Limits?

Limits are often rooted in fear, insecurity, religion, lack of trust, etc.
These limits breed low self-esteem, depression,
regrets, stagnation, and more.

Your Limits Hinder You and Displeases God

Read: 2 Corinthians 5:7; Hebrews 11:6
Think About It: In what way is your lack of
faith limiting God in your life?

_____

_____

_____

_____

_____

God Has Plans For You

Read: Jeremiah 29:11
Think About It: What plans for your life has God revealed to you?
If you do not know, ask Holy Spirit

_____

_____

_____

_____

_____

Further Thought: Has there ever been a time
you stepped out of your comfort zone?
What did it feel like? What was the result?

_____

_____

_____

_____

_____

Tying It All Together:

Life caused us to build our place of comfort and safety. All our decisions are based on the limited space the 'box' affords us. These limits hinder us from the life God planned for us. To live life according to His plans we must be willing to step out of our place of comfort and safety. We must be willing to take God initiated risks.

NOTES

You Can Only See So Far

The limits you place on yourself create a self-imposed prison.
In this prison your vision is distorted – you
view life through your limits.

You Can Be Free

Read: 2 Timothy 2:26
Think About It: How has your self-imposed prison
assisted the devil in keeping you captive?

_____

_____

_____

_____

_____

God Wants You Free

Read: Galatians 5:1
Think About It: How has your vision hindered
you from the freedom Christ has provided?

_____

_____

_____

_____

_____

Further Thought: What are some changes
you need to make to live free?

_____

_____

_____

_____

_____

Tying It All Together:

Limits create a self-imposed prison. *There* you view life through the blurred vision of fear. The fear of being hurt, disappointed and betrayed - again. To see life more clearly you must view it from God's perspective. From His perspective you view life through the lens of love rather than fear.

NOTES

Seeing Through God's Eyes

When God looks at you, He sees where you are
now, but He also knows His plans for you.
When God allows us to see or hear about our
future He does so without limits.

Doubt Blocks Our Vision

Read: Proverbs 3:5; Matthew 13:3-6
Think About It: In what ways are you rejecting the *seeds* of God's
promises because you are *leaning* to your own understanding?

_____

_____

_____

_____

_____

God Forms [shapes, molds] Us Based On His Plans

Read: Isaiah 64:8; Philippians 2:13
Think About It: Identify some areas God is currently *forming* you?

_____

_____

_____

_____

_____

Further Thought: If you were whole emotionally, your esteem balanced, your identity sure, and your value [worth] known aka living free, how would your life look? What would you be doing differently?

_____

_____

_____

_____

_____

Tying It All Together:

God does not create a plan for you when you accept Christ into your heart. His plans for you began in your mother's womb. As he knitted you together the plans were being laid. Where you are in life does not matter. The decisions made to get there are irrelevant. Through all you have endure the plans of God for you remained the same.

NOTES

Who Are You Surrounded By?

It matters who is around you.
We often surround ourselves with like-minded
people – there is no risk in this.

You Must Be Willing To Disconnect

Read: Matthew 4:19; Galatians 5:9
Think About It: Who are you holding on to that
God has called you to disconnect from? Why?

_____

_____

_____

_____

_____

God Wants More For You

Read: Ephesians 3:20
Think About It: Why are you holding on to
the negative people in your life?

_____

_____

_____

_____

_____

Further Thought: How are the people around
you supporting your God-inspired goals?

_____

_____

_____

_____

_____

Tying It All Together:

The influence of those around you impacts your life more than you
realize. We unknowingly surround ourselves with other like-minded
people. They often look like you, talk like you, and share the same inter-
ests, morals, and values as you. This is not an accident. This is by design
to keep you locked in your box - your place of limits. We must embrace
that God knows best, even in our relationships.

NOTES

The Failure To Communicate

God will allow those around you to see *glimpses*
of His desires (plans) for you.
In most cases they cannot explain it because it is *foreign* to them.

The Nay-Sayers And Doubters

Read: Numbers 13:31-33
Think About It: What is the response when you
share your God-ideas with those around you?

_____

_____

_____

_____

_____

You Keep Sharing With Them

Read: 1 Corinthians 15:33
Think About It: Why do you continue to share
your God-ideas with those around you?

_____

_____

_____

_____

_____

Further Thought: One can only give you
what they have and so much of it.
How does this statement apply to the people you lean on for support?

_____

_____

_____

_____

_____

Tying It All Together:

One cannot properly explain what they do not have the language for. It would be like an American in France requesting tacos. The request would get lost in translation. This is what happens when you share your faith-filled God-ideas with those around you. Most times they cannot relate to what you are saying. Rather than encourage you to move in it, they discourage, downplay and/or ridicule your dreams. Their inability to give you the words you need to move forward can keep you in cycles and limits.

NOTES

You Cannot Rescue You

By now your eyes are opening to the limits you have placed on yourself. You may be realizing your way is keeping you from moving forward.

You Are Making Plans Without God

Read: Proverbs 16:9

Think About It: How have you been 'doing life' without God? What is the result?

_____

_____

_____

_____

You Are Trying To Make It Happen In Your Own Strength

Read: 2 Corinthians 9:12

Think About It: Compared to God's limitless resources, what resources do you have?

_____

_____

_____

_____

Further Thought: Many believe, "I got myself
into this, I can get myself out of it."
How has this way of thinking delayed you
breaking cycles and patterns in your life?

_____

_____

_____

_____

_____

Tying It All Together:

By now your eyes are opening to the cycles you are living in. You should be taking a true assessment of your patterns of behavior. The main thing you should be grasping is your inability to rescue yourself. If you could, you would have done so years ago. Now is the time for you to accept that you need God to get you out of that which you are stuck in.

For I know the plans I have for you, says the LORD. They are plans for good and not for evil, to give you a future and a hope.

Jeremiah 29:11 TLB

God Will Remember His Promises/Plans Concerning You

You may have forgotten what God said about you, but God has not.
The release of the promises/plans for life are for a predetermined time.

God's Promises/Plans Bring Joy To Your Life

Read: Proverbs 14:12-13
Think About It: How often do you feel sad and/or depressed?
Knowing God desires joy for you, what are you
willing to change to experience it daily?

_____

_____

_____

_____

You Must Be Ready For Change – God's Way

Read: Exodus 2:23
Think About It: The Children of Israel cried
out to God because of their bondage.
They were desperate for change. How desperate for change are you?

_____

_____

_____

_____

Further Thought: Do you believe God responds
to your prayers? Why or why not?

_____

_____

_____

_____

_____

Tying It All Together:

God responds to a desperate cry. The cry of desperation is a loud cry one makes when a situation is so bad you are willing to do anything to get out of it. This is not a reaction and/or an emotional cry. It is a cry that lets Him know you are ready to do things *His* way.

NOTES

God Will Come *See* About You

God hears the cries of His people.
He knows when they are (really) ready for His promises.

When God Looks At You, He Acknowledges You As Well

Read: Exodus 2:25
Think About It: In what ways have you have
identified God acknowledging you?

_____

_____

_____

_____

_____

God Works Behind The Scenes

Read: Exodus 3:8
Think About It: In what ways are you showing
God you trust He is working in your life?

_____

_____

_____

_____

_____

Further Thought: "Any way you bless me LORD I'll be satisfied"
How true is this statement in your life?

_____

_____

_____

_____

_____

Tying It All Together:

We often believe God has forgotten us because of the hardships of life. We forget that God's promises for our life are for a predetermined time. This predetermined time is not based on *our* timeline or schedule. He works in our life in tandem with His overall plan for the world. The key to successfully waiting is to do so patiently while trusting that God is working.

NOTES

God Can... God Will Rescue You

Most believe God based on their five senses.
Many believe God based on their experiences with Him.

God Can - Most Believe This

Read: Exodus 4:29-31
Think About It: What have you witness that
lets you know God can do anything?

_____

_____

_____

_____

God Will For Me - Many Struggle Believing This

Read: Exodus 5:21
Think About It: Why do you struggle believing
God will come through for you?

_____

_____

_____

_____

Further Thought: How would you describe
your trust and belief in God.

_____

_____

_____

_____

_____

Tying It All Together:

Many believe God can do anything. However, they struggle with trusting *He will* for them. Often this is because of our wrongdoings, our disobedience to His will and ways. We must gain confidence in the truth that God's love for us is not conditional. He loves us because He *is* love. And He blesses us because of that.

NOTES

You Must Come Out

Many have their idea of how God will bring them out.
We must be open to His plan of rescue.

You Struggle With God's Way

Think About It: Based on your experience,
how does God work in your life?

_____

_____

_____

_____

You Struggle With God's Plan

Think About It: How has your ideas
hindered God's plans for your life?

_____

_____

_____

_____

__Further Thought__: What is God requiring of you
to break free from the cycles in your life?

_____

_____

_____

_____

_____

Tying It All Together:

Our thoughts about how God will free us from bondage is often a grand
affair. It is something to be seen by all. It will 'show *them* a thing or two
about who I am'. They will regret ever messing with me. While this may
be fun to think about, it is not God's way. At least not in the manner we
think of it. When He brings us out it is not for our glory, but for His.
God does it in a way that ensures He will get all the accolades for how it
was accomplished. He will get all praise for doing it for you.

NOTES

You Must Be Decided

Freedom does not equal immediate promise.
You must continue through the process.

The Wilderness Season(s)

Read: Exodus 13:17-18
Think About It: What do you think of when
you hear Wilderness Season?

_____

_____

_____

_____

_____

Keep Moving Forward

Read: Exodus 14:15
Think About It: How determined are you to see the process through?

_____

_____

_____

_____

_____

Further Thought: Where do believe God is taking you?

_____

_____

_____

_____

_____

Tying It All Together:

When God breaks you free from bondage, He does not give you imme-diate access to the promise. He will allow time for rest and refreshment to reflect on what *just* happened. This is designed to encourage you to continue the journey. Once your strength is renewed, He takes you through a process of healing and deliverance - the wilderness season. This is needed so you will not mishandle the promises when you receive them. Before starting out, you must decide to see the process through - NO MATTER WHAT!

NOTES

The Journey To Healing Begins

The more submitted you are to the process, the easier it will be.
Focusing on *your* process limits disappointments.

The Inner-Work

Read: Psalm 26:2; 139:23-24
Think About It: What would you say is the condition of your heart?

_____

_____

_____

_____

_____

A New You

Read: 2 Corinthians 3:18
Think About It: How do you see yourself?
Be as detailed as possible.

_____

_____

_____

_____

_____

Further Thought: Patience with the process and patience with self are keys to success on this journey. What is your current patience level with processes and yourself?

_____

_____

_____

_____

_____

Tying It All Together:

How long will it take? This is the universal question when starting on a journey? On this trip the answer to this question is entirely up to you. The more submitted you are to the process, the quicker and easier it is to endure. Defiance, denial and (self) deception will cause the journey to be long and drawn much more than planned. Eliminating comparison while focusing on *your* process limits disappointments, confusion, and further delay. Patiently enjoy the journey while learning more about yourself and God.

NOTES

DAY 14

What Is Faith?

Faith is the main ingredient – it is like flour for a cake.
Faith is the fuel that is pushing you forward.

Now Faith Is...

Read: Hebrews 11:1
Think About It: How do you define faith?

_____

_____

_____

_____

_____

Faith Pleases God

Read: Hebrews 11:6
Think About It: How would you describe your level of faith?

_____

_____

_____

_____

_____

Further Thought: Based on your response
above, how are you living by faith?

_____

_____

_____

_____

_____

Tying It All Together:

Faith is the fuel that pushes you toward your hope (dreams, desires). It is trust or confidence in God… the foundation of our hopes. Faith is the proof of what we have discerned in the spirit-realm. It boldly declares, "It's already done!" Since this is the case, we live, speak, and act based on *this* belief.

But without faith it is impossible to please Him, for he who comes to God must believe that He is, and that He is a rewarder of those who diligently seek Him.

Hebrews 11:6

What Is Walking By Faith

It is crazy until it happens ~ *Mike Todd*

Believing Beyond What You See

Read: 2 Corinthians 5:7
Think About It: If *you* can figure it out it is not faith.
What changes do you need to make in how you walk by faith?

_____

_____

_____

_____

_____

You Must Press

Read: Philippians 3:14
Think About It: What are some reasons you have
given up on your goals and/or desires?

_____

_____

_____

_____

_____

Further Thought: Have you ever put all your trust
in God and walked by faith for something?
What did it feel like? What was the result?

_____

_____

_____

_____

_____

Tying It All Together:

To walk by faith is to walk with the confidence... the knowing that what was received from Holy Spirit whether in prayer, via prophecy and/or the written word is already done. This is accomplished by making decisions that will align one with what was seen and/or heard. We adjust our surroundings, obtain the knowledge, and continue declaring the words of God concerning us. We do all this with the assurance of the result; despite what others may think or say.

NOTES

Prayer Time - Building Relationship With The LORD

Prayer is giving our attention to God.
In prayer we are speaking to God as well as listening to Him.

Prayer Gives Our Soul A Place To Speak

Read: 1Peter 5:6-7
Think About It: How do you spend your time
in prayer? Do you speak freely?

_____

_____

_____

_____

Prayer Teaches Us The Ways of God

Read: Exodus 33:13; Psalm 25:9, 27:11
Think About It: Do you believe God speaks to you? Why or why not?

_____

_____

_____

_____

Further Thought: In what ways can your prayers be enhanced?

_____

_____

_____

_____

_____

Tying It All Together:

Prayer is the intimate time we spend giving our attention to God. In prayer we speak to Him about the things we are concerned about, the burdens we are carrying and the hidden desires of our heart among other things. We should also be listening for God to speak to us about these as well as what He desires to teach us. As we speak and listen to the LORD, His ways become more familiar to us. We learn to recognize His presence and His voice. I want to encourage you to put away your grocery list of prayers. Come to Him with an open heart and mind to receive Him daily.

NOTES

Your Mind Must Be Renewed

This should not be avoided.
The old mindset will be a hindrance in your new.

Renewing The Mind Is A Requirement

Read: Romans 12:2
Think About It: How would define 'renewing the mind'?

_____

_____

_____

_____

_____

Your Mind Must Be Properly Set

Read: Romans 8:5
Think About It: What do you think about most?

_____

_____

_____

_____

_____

Further Thought: What guides your thoughts - emotions, the past, tv, etc.?

_____

_____

_____

_____

_____

Tying It All Together:

You cannot go into your new with the old mindset. For most their thought process is rooted in disappointment, rejection, and abandonment to name a few. These *wounds* keep them from living their God-planned life. If their mind is not renewed for the new, they will find themselves back in cycles and limits. One will find that as their mind is renewed new habits will form, their thoughts will be more optimistic, and their decision making will be done with ease. This too is an area we must yield to Holy Spirit's working in our lives.

NOTES

Building Up Your Faith

Faith grows... increases over time.
We need faith to operate in the Kingdom of God.

Unbelief Is A Faith Blocker

Read: Matthew 17:20
Think About It: How often do you struggle with unbelief?

_____

_____

_____

_____

_____

The Hall of Faith

Read: Hebrews 11:3-35
Think About It: How do these acts of faith encourage you?

_____

_____

_____

_____

_____

Further Thought: How has your faith grown
since becoming a follower of Jesus Christ?

_____

_____

_____

_____

_____

Tying It All Together:

Faith is one of the keys in the Kingdom of God. It pleases Him. Why? Because when we move in faith, we are displaying our confidence and trust in God. Just like love is an action word, faith is too. Understand, faith grows... increases over time. Each time God proves Himself by doing, revealing, or confirming something our faith increases. Know this, living by faith is a fight. The enemy knows the power of it, so he fights against us to steal, kill, and destroy it every chance he gets. We oppose the enemy by keeping in remembrance all that God has done for us already. In this way we are casting down imaginations that exalts itself against the knowledge of God's will. It is God's will that we live by faith.

NOTES

Stay Focus - Keep Your Eyes On The LORD

Life, as you have known it, is changing.
You need God to lead you on this new path.

Things Are Changing

Read: Matthew 14:22-33
Think About It: How well do you adapt to change… doing new things?

_____

_____

_____

_____

_____

You Are Being Reestablished

Read: Proverbs 16:3
Think About It: What are your thoughts about
the changes coming to your life?

_____

_____

_____

_____

_____

Further Thought: Think of a time you
stepped out of your comfort zone.
How did it feel? Did you retreat when things became
overwhelming? What was the result?

_____

_____

_____

_____

Tying It All Together:

Stepping out of your place of comfort is never easy. The unknown can be intimidating. For many the fear of the unknown keeps them in their self-imposed prisons. When one leaves their comfort zone, they need God to lead them on their new path. Without Him they will quickly retreat to the familiar. We keep our eyes on the LORD by praying, reading, and meditating on the word. As you do this daily you will find yourself growing closer to the LORD as well.

NOTES

You Are Not Alone

You may feel lonely, but you are not alone.
God *IS* with you.

Valley Moments

Read: Psalm 23:4
Think About It: Do you believe God is with you? Why or why not?

_____

_____

_____

_____

_____

Fear Makes You Feel Alone

Read: Joshua 1:9
Think About It: How do you handle moments when you feel alone?
How did fear play a role?

_____

_____

_____

_____

_____

Further Thought: Many confuse the definitions of lonely and alone. Look up the words to confirm their definition. Is it different from your definition? How?

_____

_____

_____

_____

_____

Tying It All Together:

On this new path there will be times you may will feel alone. The you, you are becoming may not fit well in the old places you stepped out of. What you are feeling is not aloneness, it is loneliness. Understand, when in relationship with Christ, you are never alone. He has given the Holy Spirit to walk with us. In those moments of feeling lonely talk with Him; in doing so you will find yourself being strengthened, helped, and upheld by His righteous right hand.

NOTES

Divine Connections

New relationships are coming.
God has individuals waiting to connect with you.

God Knows What You Need

Read: Genesis 2:18
Think About It: God recognizes our need for human connection.
How well do you connect with new people?

_____

_____

_____

_____

_____

You Must Be Prepared

Read: Acts 8:26-40
Think About It: How ready are you to connect
with those outside of your norms?
For example, those of a different race, economic status, education level, etc.

_____

_____

_____

_____

_____

Further Thought: How ready are you for change?

_____

_____

_____

_____

_____

Tying It All Together:

A divine connection can be described as a God-led encounter that impacts your life. They can bring change, direction and/or understanding. As you journey on this new path you find yourself encountering people, opportunities and experiences that can only be explained as a divine connection. These moments will happen at just the right time. Regarding relationships, they may be for a moment, a season or for a lifetime. However long it lasts, I strongly suggest you enjoy the time you have with that person. Embrace the wisdom shared and learn the entire lesson.

This is My command: be strong and courageous. Never be afraid or discouraged because I am your God, the Eternal One, and I will remain with you wherever you go.

Joshua 1:9 Voice

Closing Thoughts

You Made It!!

Congratulations on completing the journey thus far!

How does it feel? How do *you* feel?

No more questions, I promise!

I know the walk may not have been easy for you at times. Having passed this way before I know how difficult facing yourself can be. Answering the tough questions, facing the (bad) experiences we tucked away, and all the other emotions that can come up is like walking through a rough terrain.

Prayerfully this journal has empowered you to continue your *Journey to Freedom*. Whether you realize it or not this is your contribution to breaking generational curses in your bloodline. As you break them, generational blessings are being established for you and future generations. Therefore, stepping out of our places of comfort is so important. Our sacrifice sets a new measure for our families. New hope, vision and ways of thinking and doing are being formed. This is also why the enemy fights against so hard.

I pray you continue your *Journey to Freedom*. I am confident you are beginning to experience the blessings that come with staying on the course. Do not forget the process is not a one-time thing. It goes way beyond the days it took you to complete this portion of the journey. Do not allow this to discourage you. Rather let it encourage you to keep fighting for your destiny and your family. The Holy Spirit has much work to do in all of us. It is all a part of the process of becoming like Christ.

Well, I leave you here. Go back through the book when needed to gain refreshment, reminders and refuel as you continue your journey. You will find yourself maturing in the things of God as you do so. The ways you used to think will be washed away. New relationships will have replaced those you lost in the early stages. Lastly, your confidence in God will have grown immensely.

Would you like to share your testimony? Email me: 21dayfreeyomind@gmail.com

Your Friend In Christ,

Jacque Jaye

About the Author

Jacque Jaye is a dedicated woman of faith who believes in God. As a diligent student of the Bible, she takes pleasure in sharing her insights with others. Currently, Jacque Jaye conducts daily sessions at 6 AM US CST on Facebook, where she provides encouragement and guidance in accordance with the teachings of the LORD. Her mission is to help individuals break free from recurring cycles and patterns that influence their decision-making and overall life. Jacque Jaye aims to remove obstacles that hinder the realization of God's plans for individuals, aspiring to see everyone live according to their divinely intended purpose.

www.ingramcontent.com/pod-product-compliance
Lightning Source LLC
Chambersburg PA
CBHW051227120626
46547CB00013B/1534